Scribbles From an Overly Caffeinated Mother

Krys Brown

BookLeaf Publishing

India | USA | UK

Presentation by *BookLeaf Publishing*

Web: www.bookleafpub.com

E-mail: info@bookleafpub.com

ISBN: 9789358312522

First edition 2023

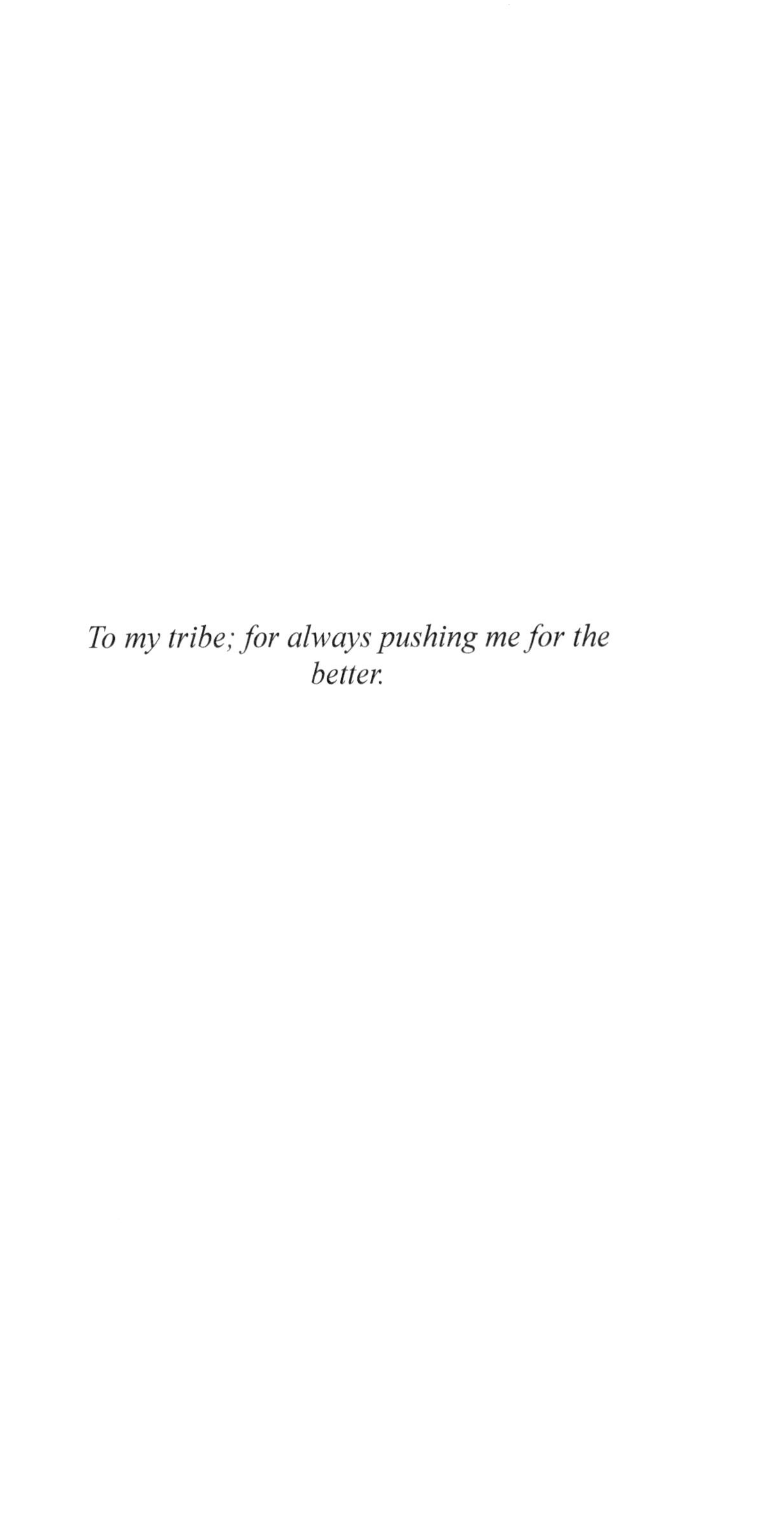

To my tribe; for always pushing me for the better.

The Rise

Before, she stayed at home.
She cooked, she cleaned,
She worked out, she baked.
The perfect Susie Homemaker.
Dinner on the table, 6 o'clock sharp.
Hair perfect, body perfect,
Dinner perfect, kids perfect.
Picture perfect in their ticky tacky suburb.
It was all about keeping up with the Jones'.
Putting her face on every morning,
She longed to do something better with her life.
To have more duty than just a house wife.
A teacher. A doctor. An artist. ANYTHING.
So behind closed doors, she cried at night.
Unremarked, unhappy, unfulfilled…

Turning to the bottle, she drank her woes away.
Hoping they would wash away like the burnt
cheese on her Pyrex.
She powdered her nose and covered up bruises
her husband left behind.
She took the hatred and anger out on her
children.
Her daughter, the most, until she was old enough
to run.

In a fit of rage, her most prized tea kettle hit the
pristine tile floor.
When she cleaned up the broken glass, she
thought to herself;

"How can she push her daughter to go for her
dreams when she failed to do that for herself?"

Her daughter, she grew up.
Her life is surrounded by
The uproar of new music.
She lived her days with peace in her heart,
Loved harder than she ever knew growing up,
And engulfed herself in the hippie lifestyle.
She hitch hiked her way through life.
Like a leaf in the wind, without a care in the
world.

She loved her lumpy love body like it was a
work of art.
Low self conscious with high self esteem,
She danced her way through life, naked and
unafraid.
That work of art was eventually put up against a
wall,
Nailed with bruises and broken trust.
She found herself beating all odds after she,
herself, was beaten.

With a questionable past, and a resume to make
your grandmother blush, she found her way
here.

After too much sex, drugs, and rock'n'roll, the
daughter gives her mother a grandchild.
Another girl but it brought up in the dawn of
technology.

Me.
I grew up to the sound of vinyl,
Feeling the soft green grass beneath my feet,
And with the lingering smell of stale cigarette
smoke.
I saw laserdisc turn into dvds right before my
turntable eyes.
Windows 95 to Windows 10, waiting hours,
minutes, seconds for a download.
I found my soul sister before google found me.
Chat rooms, limewire, and cyber bullying.
You get the gist, I'm a 90's kid.
Typical life, but nothing actually given for free.

I've been to small get togethers and out of hand
parties.
I've walked the dark streets of downtown as a
young teen,
With money in my pockets I said I needed for
the movies,

Just to get into the local punk scene.

Eventually, through life, I met this gorgeous
man.
Ya know, with strong arms and a tan.
We were so inseparable and so in-love.
Quickly after a positive test,
I learned he was a narcissist, manipulative, and
emotionally abusive.
I knew how to handle physical abuse from the
stories I'd been told.
But what do you do with this?
He never hit me, only broke things,
Dishes and trinkets, but mostly electronics.
Through family, I finally gained the courage to
cut him out…

Now I have a daughter.
I want her to grow up strong and sure of herself,
To trust that gut feeling even when it scares the
hell out of her.
To be the hippie wild child I know she'll always
be.
To dance and sing like no one is watching.
To be the queen of everything.
You best believe she'll know how to change her
own oil,
And put on those winter tires, because

She'll be taught that you don't need a partner to
take care of you,
That no one puts their hands on you,
That no one who loves you will make you feel
terrible about yourself.
That your voice needs to be heard, even when it
shakes.
That no matter the time, if you want it bad
enough, it will be yours.
That if the door keeps shutting, find a window to
go through.
Only you are responsible for you.
Chin up buttercup, the world is your oyster.
And don't ever settle for less than you deserve,
And baby girl, you deserve the world.

Faults

It's your fault.
It comes with an automatic negative
connotation.
It's your fault;
That you ruined that perfect outfit.
That you left the coffee pot on and it's burned.
That you misheard something and refused to see
it another way.
That you forget the simplest things.
That they misheard you and got feelings hurt.
That sometimes it's too hard to see the silver
lining when the cloud is too big.
However; it comes with a positive.

It's your fault;
That I wouldn't be the same person without you.
That you spread joy everywhere you go.
That I think of you every time I order Starbucks.
That we have so many inside jokes.
"Remember that one time.."

It's your fault;
That you have so many inside jokes with so
many people.

That they too think of you when something
comes up.
It's your fault;
That you don't realize how truly amazing you
are.
That you've touched lives without realizing it.
That you are an incredible woman, a passionate
wife, and a beautiful daughter.

When I was four, I pleaded with my parents for a
sister.
Little to my knowledge, she was right down the
block waiting for me.
It's your fault that you're an extraordinary
awesmoe soul sister,
And I wouldn't have it any other way.

Sister (1 of 6)

(I was supposed to perform this at a local poetry slam contest with a sister but covid happened and kept me from doing so. Please enjoy.)

I am the middle child, literally.
But I'm the oldest of the youngest.
I have too many siblings to count.
Pick one, any one. How about that one?

The one with the crip stick, the pimp limp, and the most contagious laugh you've ever heard.
Porcelain skin, jet black hair, and glamorous make up we shared in the war room.
Full of poetic brilliance, she could fill a stage on just bravado alone.
Nerves go crazy being up here, but she's one of the strongest women I know.
You could never tell through that smile of hers that we've lost two siblings in the last 10 years.
Or that it took many spoons to be here tonight, to enjoy this, because of an engine in her lap.

Full of inspiration, random facts, and crafty as all get out.

We push each other for the better, and even
Wyatt our way into some shenanigans.
We've, well, she's taken out displays at Target
while we let my child run crazy.
She's stubborn as hell. Don't tell her she won't
do something, because she will.
I learned that the hard way with her cane and my
shin.

She has always talked me down from my tree as
I've tried to keep her head afloat.
Even with ALL the shit she's been through, I
know I can always count on her.
Hell, I don't know who I would be now without
her here today.
When I need advice, to vent, or to just simply
swim in ALL the tea.
She's always there. Ready to listen and offer a
hug or three.

Besides a sister, she's an incredible aunt. The
founder of the Elite Auntie Alliance.
There's more than just my daughter, we have a
cousin crew.
She's the pied piper of the children and keeps
them in line.
But also opens the door to someone that they
trust and can come to with their worst problems.

I appreciate what she does for our littles and everything in between.

When I was younger, I wanted a sister. A baby sister.
But then I got married into this crazy household I now call family.
I lucked out and got both. A little, and big sisters.

Telephone

I would rather coyote ugly my arm than pick up
an unknown call.
There's always small talk and an awkward
goodbye.
What do they want, I surely don't have a script
for this.
I don't remember, maybe I'll text them to
confirm.

My Mom left for the hospital,
Something happened something is wrong.
We carry on in anticipation for the call..
Our traditional Christmas Eve spaghetti dinner
was especially good that year.

I repeatedly denied it while sobbing into the
phone,
Joining in my cries, my sisters blanketed
themselves around me.
We called and rerouted everyone, while we
headed out ourselves,
"I love you" was the last thing cried through the
phone each time.
I can at least live knowing that was the last thing
I said to him before I said goodbye forever.

Zoë Raen

My sweet summer child,
My Gemini first born,
The trial run.

Thank you for growing up with me,
I've learned to love myself in loving you.
My carbon copy.

Born from an accident but raised with purpose,
You're creative, and headstrong, and funny as all
hell.
You're quick on your toes and you amaze me
everyday.

When you figure out where you're going in life,
You're going to be unstoppable.
You have the confidence and a village to back
you.

I hope you fight for those who have lost their
voice;
and yes, even yours.
Stand tall, even when your hands tremble and
your voice shakes.

Words are powerful, use them wisely.
I believe in you and your generation,
Go and fuck shit up.

Luna Faye

My light in the dark,
My second born Capricorn,
Oh god, are you red headed?

Painted nails, and spinny skirts
Monster trucks and knee deep in dirt.
Princess Peach and Bubble Guppies

She is the enigma that came from me.
3 years old and ever changing.
Who knows what she'll be into next.

Always on her sister's skirt tails,
And keeping up with the cousin crew,
She came into the world like a force of nature.

I wouldn't want to fuck with her, would you?
I bet she fights dirty, just like her mother.
She knows the strength of her village, even as
the babiest.

You

Here I am, looking into eyes that aren't quite the
shade of the ocean, but I've been drowning in
them since we first met.

I'd say I'll love you unconditionally but that
Simply wouldn't be true.
Be the lighthouse I need when the storm is
getting too rough.
Be my shade when the sun is burning down on
us and the cover for when it rains.
Forever fill my cup as I will yours and we shall
never drink alone.

I have laughed so hard my cheeks have hurt.
I've cried so hard I've left water marks and snot
strings on your collar.
I'm so happy I get to do that for the rest of my
life.

Thank you for being there on my brightest days
and my darkest.

Me

Ima mother, a daughter, a sister, an aunt.
Ima lover, a fighter, a grinner, and a sinner.
Caffeine is my drug of choice,
oui'd for fun, and drink to let loose.
I refuse to become my mother.

I have many interests with no desire for any.
A struggling artist without a muse.
No motivation, or inspiration
Even finding words now, is difficult

It could be the depression.
I've had it awhile now and
I've just become numb to it.
This is how I am now.

Everyone always comes before me.
A poor quality I see in myself.
Thanks to trauma and care giving,
It's all hard to unlearn.

Guilt

I have 20$ toothpaste but I couldn't tell you
when I last brushed my teeth.
I don't brush my hair but because it's short
enough.
My mental health is hanging on a thread, waiting
for the hat to drop.

There's so much guilt that I feel like I'm
drowning.
The want to stay in bed is greater than the need
to get up.
My girls need me to be present so I've been
doing the minimum.

Keep the children alive.

I'm trying to do better,
Even if we're at the park at 9pm.
Even if we've gotten ice cream twice that day.
Even if all we've done is watch cartoons.

They're fed. They're happy.
But I'm not present like I should be.
Phone glued to my hand, I'm not even
productive.
I cook and I clean but I can't get in-front of it.
There's always a pile. Somewhere.

Guilt pt. 2

I can feel me pulling away from everyone.
They know somethings wrong,
And expect me to know what.
I don't know what's wrong.
But pressuring me to talk doesn't make it easier.

I struggle with on the spot conversations I
wasn't ready for.
I memorize my lines so it makes it easier to
retell.
I just don't have the energy for others right now.
I barely have enough for myself.

Body

I didn't care for chunky babies for the longest
time,
Until I had a 10 pound beautiful baby girl
I loved every inch of each roll she had on her
body.

I didn't care for the transformation my body did
after creating such an incredible person.
I've struggled with body image issues since
before her.
Always thought I needed to be a certain way,
Since that's how we are conditioned.

Watching her little body sprawled out, sound
asleep,
Made me begin to love my own body again.
Unfortunately, I internalize my thoughts so my
daughters don't inherit the same voice.

"Love your body the way your mother loved
your baby feet"
The words Mary Lambert said hit me so deep,
I no longer mention anyone's body besides how
they chose to decorate it that day.

You are more than just your body.
Love it for it is the only one you have.
Love it for it creates miracles, and brings life.

Beta Testing

You left me for Canada,
We found a note,
You left his daughter but took your son.
You blamed school and left me behind.
You left our dad for a piece of work,
Met in Diablo 2, and flew the coop.

You chose booze over food.
Who lets their kid eat uncooked hamburger
helper?
You chose cigarettes over clean air.
Do you know how often I got asked if I smoked?
You choose staying sick over a doctor.
Do you know how many times I've waited until
it was dire?
Complained about our dentist bills, but kept
feeding us candy and soda.
Who buys their freshman a case of rockstar?

You say you did everything you could,
But you could have done better.
I do what you do, and make sure my kids come
first.
Make sure they have their needs met before I
even thinking of my own.

I'm trying to curb it but when you come from
nothing..
you make sure your kids have everything.

AuDHD

Who am I?
My name is Ned.
I have a hat on my head.
Through the phone,
Through the wall,
I hear nothing on the line, at all.

My script is song lyrics, book lines and tv
quotes.
I talk better with memes and gifs.
I'm particular about things that don't make
sense.
I do things a certain way because it's better.

I have a cereal bowl, a ramen bowl, and a
favorite fork.
I don't like water, my mind is messy, please fold
this for me.
Microfiber and corduroy make my skin crawl,
don't get me started on velvet.

I'm overwhelmed easy, sometimes.
The screaming is fine but the music needs to go.
Why is someone always touching me?

I've heard my name 6 thousand times, and you
don't need a thing.

Can I poop in peace?
Is dinner almost done?
Fuck this never ending laundry.
I can get mad easily over stupid things.
Some lights are harsh, deep bass hurts.
Please stop chewing so loud!

Ima disassociate til time passes.
I have appointments but nothing to do.
I have so many projects I'm working on.
Ask me when I'm doing laundry why I'm now
cleaning the bathroom and going through old
junk?

These clothes are too tight in all the wrong
places.
Nail files make my ears itch.
There's a rock in my shoe.
There's a hole in my sock,
And I'm twiddling it with my toes.

And all I can think is
What is wrong with me?

Friendship

As told by Urban Dictionary*

- Giving up pizza to save a life, no questions asked
- Munching on a well cooked face together
- Not wanting to change anything about them
- A mutual bond of trust of personal feelings, and experiences
- Loving someone with every ounce of your being
- Genuinely wanting them happy even if it means sacrificing your own
- When your love for them exceeds your need for them
- Becoming closer after discussing agreements
- And loving each other more afterwards
- Someone you don't have to talk to but want to
- Always listening, and someone to cry on or seek advice from

Simply, Magic

Virgo

She's my sign,
I know her as well as she knows herself
We feed on each other's empathy
I can tell what she's feeling by just a glance
Just as she does mine
Though I feel like I hide mine better.

Those green eyes of hers
Have seen struggle, violence, and hatred.
However, they've also seen tenderness, passion
and joy.

Moon lit beaches make her wild,
Sun soaked skin mellows her senses.
Nocturnal and infinitely creative.

She's been through hell and back,
Just to continue to say "is that all you got?"

Rose

Red flags look like flags when wearing rose
colored glasses.

Twitterpation, infatuation, puppy love.
The honey moon stage in which no one can do
wrong.
Inseparable, entangled in one another, blind to it
all.

I've played capture the flag one too many times,
I know what I'm looking for,
And what to avoid to not get caught up in the
game.

I've run out of lens cleaner trying to ensure I'm
seeing clearly.
That the flags are in fact.. just flags.
When do the rose colored glasses become.. just
glasses?

I'm happy, genuinely happy.
It pains me immensely from smiling entirely
quite too much.
My hesitant, apprehensive self resisted the fall
on our first meeting.
You calmed my crazy hurricane of a mind.
How does one not fall..into the eye of the storm?

Deaf

I require hearing aids.
Do I wear them? No.
Was it the countless ear infections I had as a
child?
Or was it the loud music?

How else was I going to drown out the noise?
All I could hear was someone else's TV and
raspy chain smoker yells between two
alcoholics.

Left to my devices,
I sing my voice hoarse
With music too loud,
I drown out myself as well.

As an adult,
I hear bits and pieces of things.
Mostly I hear them correctly,
But I also never hear the right thing.

I still listen to music loud.
I need to feel it too.
My ears ring with intensity.
They drown out soft moments I wish to partake.

I should wear my hearing aids.

Hell Month

Out of the 12, one is hell.
Though it starts and ends with a birthday,
It's filled with reminders of death.
I barely have enough holiday cheer for my
children

I used to get it after birthdays were done
But two siblings, a death day and a birthday
And one of an alcoholic mother who's wasting
away
Are weighing on my cheery demeanor.

I'm hoping one day Santa leaves some in my
stocking,
I'm saving what I have for my kids.

=^..^=

To be a kitten,
Lazy and warm
Found in any sunspot
Playful and curious
Lost in a delivery box

No job
No schedule
Nothing but
Soft fur
Head skritches
And cute toe beans

I long to be the kitten
Sleeping in the sun.

To Read or To Be Read

Ziggity Zaggity Zoom
There's room on the broom
For friends like you
Bubble bubble pasta pot
Make my pasta nice and hot
Be careful who you return coupons to,
Because SHES NOT A WITCH!

Even that Jim we hate will help us hide,
Llama llama drama llama
Emily Elizabeth encouraging shenanigans,
Frog and Toad, the best of friends
Winnie the Pooh and Tigger too,
You never know who will come next.

There's a cat in the hat on a wacky Wednesday
He speaks for the trees while counting out fish.
It's not easy being a bunny,
But the best nest is NOT on a bell.
I'd rather have duck feet than be a bull frog.
It's a great day for UP but I'm not getting up
today.

You can't catch me Seuss, I'm the gingerbread
man!

Keep the leprechaun from messing up the
school.
Stand tall Molly Lou Melon,
don't put up with this fool!
I wanted to help,
just for you, but
We all play together like peanut butter and
cupcake.